THE
FIGHT
OF MY
LIFE

LATRICIA JACOBS

All scripture quotations noted ESV are taken from THE ENGLISH STANDARD VERSION. Crossway Bibles. (2007). ESV: Study Bible: English Standard Version. Wheaton, III Crossway Bibles.
All scripture quotations noted KJV are taken from THE KING JAMES VERSION. Dallas, TX: Brown Books Publishing. (2004). The Holy Bible: King James Version. Brown Books Publishing.
All scripture quotations noted NKJV are taken from the NEW KING JAMES VERSION. Nashville: Thomas Nelson. (1982). Used by permission. All rights reserved.
All scripture quotations noted NASB are taken from the NEW AMERICAN STANDARD BIBLE. La Habra, CA: Foundation Publications, for the Lockman Foundation. (1971). Used by permission. All rights reserved.
All scripture quotations noted NLT are taken from the NEW LIVING TRANSLATION. Tyndale House Publishers. (2004). Holy Bible: New Living Translation. Wheaton, III: Tyndale House Publishers. Used by permission. All rights reserved.
ISBN: 978-0-578-69528-0

THE FIGHT OF MY LIFE

DEDICATION

This book is dedicated to my daughters:

Never quit queens. Know your worth. Never give up on your fight, because it's fixed; and you're worth fighting for. God has already designed it and Jesus has already paid the price for your victory. No matter what test, trials, or tribulations you face; know that God already knows about them, and he promises never to leave or forsake you. Not even death can separate his love from you. Thank you both for your love, support and transparency. Most importantly, for sharing me with others and understanding the call that's on my life.

I love you two forever!

Mom

LETTER TO MY SISTER

Nicole (my keeper),

I don't have many regrets in life, but I regret not being my best for you as we were growing up. Thank you for always loving me, despite the way I treated you at times. Although we were kids, I could've done better. Please accept my apology, and thank you for giving me another opportunity to really be a big sister to you.

Sincerely,

Missy

THE
FIGHT
OF MY
LIFE

LATRICIA JACOBS

Round 1

"The Fight to Live"

Do you ever wonder about God? Whether he really exists? Does God love us? Does he hear our voice? Does he really have great things in store for us? What is *HIS* plan for our lives? Are we that important to God, that he wants to use us to fulfill his purpose? What is that purpose? Do we have a say so? How much is required of us? Will we come out victorious?

"Yet you brought me safely from my mother's womb and led me to trust you at my mother's breast. I was thrust into your arms at my birth. You have been my God from the moment I was born."
Psalm 22:9-10NLT

It was the spring of 1975. Gerald Ford was the President of the United States, and minimum wage was two dollars and ten cents. My grandparents had a full house, with six children of their own. My mom Cassandra included. She was the eldest of six all beautiful, fair skinned children, with long wavy hair. At the tender age of fourteen she was pregnant with me, and I was on the way. Knowing my grandmother's personality, I still try to figure out how my mom and I both survived. I know the struggle for my grandparents was real. My grandmother housed and helped care for her mother, her siblings, and her cousin's most of the time. Her house was always full. She did her best to ensure that everyone was fed, comfortable, and could call her house home. I truly thank God that my grandmother did not force my mother to abort my life's journey. Although I can't help but wonder how she must've felt, when she received the news that my mother was expecting at such a young age. Did she feel at fault, ashamed or even heartbroken, when she received the news? I guess I'll never know, because I never asked her. I just wish that I had the same boldness, courage, and strength that my grandmother did when I found myself in a similar situation.

I must confess, I felt I missed the mark and fell short of God's glory; when I was faced with a similar situation. I lived in guilt for such a long time, because of the things I had done. Things that I tried to keep out of sight, and out of my mind. I was hoping that those things would never be discovered. I tried to leave it all behind, only to find out later in life that being transparent about my guilt would not only help me; but would also help others to become free from shame, guilt and self-hatred. People need to know that they're not alone. We don't get it right all the time. We all fall short at some point in our lives. When we can learn from our shortcomings, we become better people than we were before. We all have said or even done some things we weren't proud of. It took me some time to realize, that the more I kept things hidden under the rug, the more I was troubled and made troubling decisions. Not being able to discuss things that happened to me, really bothered me. How can we really receive help for the things that we keep hidden? Can we honestly say that trouble won't last always, if we never uncover and deal with the trouble? There are ways that may appear to be right in our eyes, but when we don't learn from our mistakes it can lead to destruction and ruin our lives.

"There is a way that seems right to a man, But its end is the way of death."
Proverbs 14:12NKJV

On Friday, April 25, 1975 at approximately 6:20am, I arrived. Three months before I was due. As a premature newborn, the doctors projection was that I would die and not live. I can truly imagine how my mother felt hearing those words about me. As of today in my own life, I am given the same projection from doctors regarding my mom's life after having five strokes. Yet, I remain hopeful, and grateful unto God for the breath of life. Not just for my own life, but the life that was used to bring me forth. My mother's life. As I reflect back to the day I arrived on the scene, just as my mother had told me. The doctors explained to my mother all of the obstacles I faced ahead. I weighed in at only two pounds and fourteen ounces. Some called me light weight, but my family called me the underdog. When my mother held me for the first time, she called me "a miracle." Looking into my mother's eyes, her eyes spoke *"fight baby, fight for your life"* and my heart responded with a faster and stronger heartbeat. I might have been lightweight, and even looked at as the underdog; but no matter what I weighed in at, I know now that my life is worth fighting for.

"I shall not die, BUT live, and declare the works of the LORD."
Psalm 118:17NKJV

The doctors sent my mother home with a prediction of my expiration date. My mother said she really didn't know the Lord like she does today, but she wanted me so desperately to survive. She asked God to let me live, and allow me to be her miracle baby. Meanwhile doctors advised the family to prepare, and to make plans for the worst. The longer you live you begin to understand what a plan is, according to man. *A plan* is a list of steps with details of timing, and resources used to achieve an objective to do something. I've learned that there is *"man's plan"* and then there is the *"Master's Plan."* In the *"Master's Plan"* God holds the details and the timing. His resources are unlimited. The *miracle* child was part of the *"Master's Plan."* A *miracle* is the design and divine work of God. God was the source, but my mom and dad were the resources used to bring me forth. He designed me to be the light in a dark place. He designed me to preach the gospel, and to set the captives free. He designed me to heal the brokenhearted, and to bring forth restoration. What has he designed *YOU* to do? ***Jeremiah 29:11*** "For I know the plans I have for you Missy, declares the LORD, plans to prosper you and not to harm you, plans to give you hope and a future." This scripture means so much to me. It gives me the confidence, boldness, and courage that I once was missing. God chose me. Only God knows the plans for my life. He set me apart. He has the agenda, and I'm on it. He is my leader, with great plans stored just for me. He knows the future, and he provides the agenda. I will go on to see what the end shall be. The scripture doesn't say that the plans will be fulfilled without pain, suffering, hardships, and lessons; but I know God will see me through to a glorious conclusion. This has helped me even when my personal plans have fallen through, or may not have gone the way I expected. Especially the times where I was not invited somewhere, that *I* thought that I should've been. Or the opposite, such as being where I was wanted instead of where I was needed. Only God knows where he needs you to be. My personal prayer has become Lord, allow me to be where I'm needed and not where I am wanted. I want to be a part of the *"Master's Plan."*

Round 2

"The Battle Within"

Early on in my life, I started to question my appearance. The reason that I looked different from the rest of my family. I remember when my childhood friend validated my suspicion with similar opinions of me. As a child this made me feel sad. Mostly because as a society we've been trained to think that kids are supposed to look just like their mom and dad. My mother, grandparents, uncles and aunts were all good looking fair skinned people, with long wavy hair. I wanted to look like them. After all, they are my family aren't they?

One Sunday afternoon, I decided that I was going to talk to someone about my concerns, but who could I talk to that would help me to understand? There was no better person than the Matriarch of our family, my grandmother. As I walked up the stairwell to enter into my grandmother's bedroom, I became quite nervous. For those that knew her personally, they would understand the reason for my nervousness. I stood in her doorway and she said to me "Puddin, what's on your mind?" I said in a soft voice "Grandma, why am I not your color?" "What?!" She raised her voice and said "What did you ask me?" "I just wish I was your color, I replied." "There's nothing wrong with your skin color she replied back to me." "I love your color, and you're my chocolate pudding! Don't ever desire to be something that you're not!" That was the end of that conversation. What a relief it was to know that grandma loved my dark skin. I felt her words were genuine. She was always known for speaking her truth, regardless if it hurt your feelings or not. That was grandma. I've never known her to bite her tongue. To hear those words from her, meant a lot to me. However, it just wasn't enough to reassure me. I still didn't feel fully confident in my skin. Although Grandma gave me her truth, I still felt as though something was missing. This was the moment when I realized someone was missing from my life. Perhaps someone with the same skin color as me. I now had to find the strength to fight the battle that was within, because I didn't like the skin that I was in. I often wondered what triggered these thoughts of self-dislike. As a child, I recall some of my peers saying dark skin was dirty and ugly. Maybe that's when I developed a complex about my complexion. After a while, even the gap in my teeth became an issue.

This feeling may have been more common amongst darker skinned girls during this time. I'm not for certain, but that's why I believe it's important for parents (especially fathers), to affirm how beautiful, unique, and special their children are at an early age; no matter the color of their skin. People can be mean sometimes, including children. Sometimes it may be intentional, and other times it is simply a result of ignorance. Words hurt and so does ignorance. We must teach our children the POWER of their words. Words are powerful, whether positive or negative. They have the power to prompt, propel, or paralyze.

"Death and life are in the power of the tongue: and they that love it shall eat the fruit thereof."
Proverbs 18:21KJV

My feelings of self-dislike and hurt prompted me to inquire about the missing person in my life, which was my father. I was told many negative and hurtful things about his absence. Such as he denied that I was his child, or he's this, and he's that, and so on.....I had a negative image in my head of my father based on the words of others. It was very discouraging. I felt even worse for asking about someone that denied and rejected me. Yet still there was a part of me that wanted to get to know him for myself. Although I understood some of what the family was trying to explain to me. They were trying to get me to understand that I didn't need him. That I would be taken care of, and would be just fine without him. It was his loss. This was far from the truth. Undoubtedly I was taken care of, but I was far from being just fine. In fact, the same words that were used to judge him, were the same words working against me, because I was part of him; and they said "the apple doesn't fall to far from the tree." I'm sure their intentions were to make me feel confident, but instead I felt unconfirmed. As a kid in grade school, it seemed as if everyone had a mother and their real father living in the same household, except for me. Of course this wasn't the case, but as a little girl it seemed like it. Especially amongst my friends. Having your real father in your household was a big deal. I often wondered "what was so wrong with me, that my father didn't want me?" I didn't realize or understand that there was another side of the story. Perhaps if the whole story was shared, it could've been explained to me in a way that I could understand. People that suffer from addictions most often aren't the best parents. I needed to know that maybe it wasn't about my father rejecting me, but about him being rejected himself. Abandoned and needing help before he could be a father to me.

"A dad is someone that is there for his children. A dad watches and actively participates in their lives. A dad helps them grow up, raises them, nurtures them, attends dance recitals, baseball games, and is present."

A father is more of a biological term than a role. Any boy or man can father a child, but a dad accepts responsibility and maintains the role. I know that God has made him my father for a reason, and I will be blessed for honoring him. Some may question this as I did and it took me some time for me to grasp as well... How do you truly honor someone that hasn't been there, or that has hurt you? Naturally when someone hurts you, you want them to feel some of the hurt you feel, or take accountability for causing it. When you get to the point that you trust the plans of God for your life. You realize that he used so many people as vessels who weren't considered worthy *(even ourselves);* to bring forth good gifts. It's the story behind each vessels life, that reveals the glory of God. You accept what you can't change, knowing it's in the *"Master's Plan,"* and some things don't have to be explained.

As I matured and learned more about the Grace of God, I took a few things into consideration:

1. My father was a young man when he and my mom brought me into this world.
2. My mom made a choice to be with my father during that

time.

3. My father was abandoned as a child himself. How could he know not to abandon me?
4. Being a father is honorable and rewarding. Exodus 20:12 Honor your father and mother, so that you may live long in the land the Lord your God is giving you.
5. If I only love the ones that love me how would I be any different?

The ability to love those who may have abandoned, abused, assaulted, rejected, and refused us doesn't come from our own strength or ability; but from the love of God himself. To love beyond the hurt is supernatural. My father had to overcome several obstacles in his life. Abandonment and addiction to drugs were two of the biggest. Thanks be to God for deliverance and restoration. At the age of 44, I now have the father I desired when I was a little girl. God can do anything! I love and forgive my father for the years he missed.

Round 3

"The Art of Attaining Wisdom"

As a young girl, I struggled with learning. I did ok until I had to repeat the fifth grade. That was the absolute worst thing that could've happened to me at that point in my life. Along with everything else that I was experiencing as a ten year old. I just wanted to go far away from anyone who knew me, and would see that I hadn't moved on to the next expected grade level. I could recall the teacher telling my mom that I would be held back, because I was unable to comprehend. I was so embarrassed. Rejection, self-dislike, and now I wasn't smart enough either!! Why me?!

Difficulty comprehending and retaining information. How could this possibly be when my mother was so smart? Grandma never even spoke of my mom struggling in school. My mom was a young mother, and a high school graduate. She helped all her siblings with their homework. She was very well educated, so why was I having trouble comprehending? I was constantly trying to figure out what was wrong with my brain, and why I wasn't smart like my mom. Then I remembered hearing someone mention that my father never finished school. This took me back to thinking about my biological father. A few of the things I was told about him was that he didn't know how to read or write very well, and that he didn't finish school. How is that? How do you get away with not finishing school? When I was finally able to talk to him, and he explained the reason that he didn't finish school, it all made better sense to me. My father was abandoned by his biological parents at the age of five, and left to care for himself at the age of fifteen. Therefore he was left to do whatever he needed to do to survive. He said my maternal-grandmother tried to get him into school, but without the proper information from his parents, he was unable to enroll.

Abandon: to leave someone or something behind for others to look after, especially someone or something meant to be a personal responsibility. I now see how abandonment can be exchanged, deposited, and transferred to the next generation. We sometimes never get to the root of the problem. In some cases, we may keep the cycle of abandonment going by choosing to walk around in bitterness and un-forgiveness. If we can tap into the most important aspects or practical details of things, we could receive the knowledge of how things actually began to fall apart; and receive the revelation and wisdom to break the cycle of dysfunctional behavior. Once the cycle is broken we can start rebuilding healthy relationships. Just as my father and I have. Understanding my father's past helped me to understand a part of myself. I have had a few obstacles, but I was meant to achieve in life. Once I reached high school things began to change for me. I moved around in school a lot during my earlier years. When I finally became settled and stable I became more focused, as many of my distractions were gone. Especially that demon that was robbing me of my sexuality.

I started to pray more, listen, and adhere more attentively to instruction from my teachers and peers. I excelled beyond what I imagined. I got involved in the student council, and became the Vice President. I never thought I could possibly be a leader as such. I joined other activities that I never knew would interest me, such as career education and modeling. The same girl who once didn't like the color of her skin. I had now started to become more confident in my beautiful DARK skin. It was always in the *"Master's Plan"* that I become a leader and prosper. Even when I didn't see it. Who would've thought that I would be a business woman, entrepreneur, CEO and Minister, teaching the love of God? God knew, as he knows the beginning through the end. He knew exactly what I would overcome as he calls his children overcomers.

"Intelligent people are always ready to learn. Their ears are open for knowledge."
Proverbs 18:15NLT

Round 4

"Healing From Sexual Trauma"

When my mom met my stepfather, I thought finally, I'll have a DADDY that will accept me. My mom seemed so happy, and things were happening so fast. Not just for me, but for her and our family also. The arrival of my new baby sister was so exciting. She brought so much joy to our family. I still remember the first time they allowed me to hold her. I had to sit all the way back on my Aunt Lisa's bed, and carefully hold her bottom and her little head. Shortly after my sister was born, we moved away from grandma's house *(our safe place)*, and started our new life in a new space.

That new lifestyle consisted of sexual trauma, authority, discipline and religion. Now that I'm a little older and wiser I realize that we were living in BONDAGE. The oppression, and controlling spirit had taken its toll on me. I will admit, we received some much needed structure, but some of the treatment was unfair and not expressed properly. For example, we had to stop wearing braids, jewelry, and pants. That was a big deal to me. We could no longer participate in dance recitals, folk festivals, or activities such as cheerleading, etc. There were no more visits to grandma's after church on Sunday's, and no more one on ones with me and my mother. Things became so controlled that it was depressing.
As a kid it was a big adjustment and happened so suddenly. We went from being raised by our grandmother, to a man ruling the household and everyone in it. This was a big change and I didn't understand a lot that was going on. Like the reason my mom had become quiet, and so serious. It seemed as if she changed overnight, and it was uncomfortable. As children, my sister and I couldn't really express ourselves. It didn't help that we were separated from our family and friends that we were familiar with. Nevertheless, I went from being rejected by one father, to being inappropriately desired by the next father who was entrusted to take care of me. Keeping that secret of inappropriate behaviors for

15

such a long time made me sad, miserable, and ultimately mean. Night after night I fought the same demon. The scripture *John 10:10* which reads "the thief comes to steal, kill and destroy" is what I lived each night. The enemy likes to get us isolated from the people that love and protect us, so that he can have his way. So that he can torment us.

As parents, we must ask the Lord for discernment, and wisdom. We must also stay available to our children. If I can give any advice to those with children, especially young children; it is to keep the communication flowing no matter what changes you experience in your lives. I promised myself to never let my children feel as if they're less important than any adult. We must be conscious of the people we allow access to our children. As parents, we must protect them from pedophiles and assassins sent to steal their joy. The demonic spirits sent to kill their relationships and destroy bonds.

John 10:10 concludes with, "I have come that they may have life, and that they may have it more abundantly." To me that means that when God puts a family together, and that family puts him first in life; they should have more in life. Not just of anything, but more LOVE, more guidance, and more knowledge. This may not be a perfect life, but a full and satisfying life. Some get confused about the order of the household. Sometimes decisions have to be made to focus on one person over another. We should stay in tuned with our children, for they are the next generation.

I think the hardest part for me during this time, was not being able to communicate with my grandmother. She was the one person that protected me, cared for me, and showed me favor no matter what. It was difficult to maintain the girl I once was, while having this important connection cut off. It had gotten to a point where each time I asked my mother if we could go see grandma. She would say, go ask your daddy *(my step-father)*. I already knew the end result, but I tried each time. Only to get the same answer, or rather the same questions from him that would leave me in tears. He would always ask why I needed to go there, and apparently my answer was never what he wanted to hear, or was willing to accept. Coincidently, I would always be on punishment, so that was another reason why we couldn't go visit. It was true. I was always on punishment, because we needed permission for everything.

When we did ask, the answer most likely was still a NO, so I started doing things without permission. I started rebelling against my mom, and this made things worse for me; not just for me, but for my little sister also. That's the one thing I regret until this day. Getting my sister in trouble for my rebellion. I ran away, I became mean, and I didn't care who got in trouble for it as long as it wasn't me. The saying that hurt people hurt people is true, but we don't have to stay hurt. We have a choice.

I've learned from my mistakes, and how to make peace with my past so that it wouldn't kill my present. In 2016, God started dealing with me regarding things I've said and done that may have hurt other people. One by one I reached out to them to ask for their forgiveness. I specified what I did, and how I was sorry and needed their forgiveness. There were 3 people. My sister being amongst the 3, and the closest to me. I realized that I wasn't the only victim. She was a victim also because she was right there in the same household. She endured just as much as I did, but I was blinded by my own hurt. Two others that I reached out to, were childhood friends that were really good friends to me. Due to the peer pressure of feeling like I needed to be BIG and BAD, *something that I wasn't*; I mistreated them by lying and making it seem like they were against me. It was all a big act and they were really there for me. I was the one against *myself*. It was as if I didn't want their friendship. Like it was too good to be true for them to like me for me, when I really didn't even like myself. I picked a fight with them, both at different times. I accused them of wanting to fight me.

My actions were distasteful; But God is amazing because he delivered me from myself. He will test your heart. I heard the Holy Spirit tell me to get it right with those people. Although they may have forgotten, he had not because he brought it back to my memory. I had never repented for my actions, nor had I asked them for their forgiveness. I felt my heart pounding, and I knew what I must do in order to be in good standing with God and his people. I was ready either way, to be forgiven or ignored by these people that I hadn't really spoken to since grade school; but I knew I had to be obedient. After reaching out to each one of them, their responses were different. One response was "we were kids", the other was "I've already forgiven you" and the last friend didn't recall the situation. It was fine either way, because it was still needed for my sake, integrity and freedom. God was doing something new in me. He was changing me from the inside out. From that mean and selfish person, into a loving, caring, encourager for his purpose. If he did it for me, he can do it for you too. I'm so glad I'm not the person that I once was. We have to learn to ask for forgiveness, and not use the trauma we went through as an excuse to mishandle people. When we know better; we should do better, not just for us, but as an example for the next generation. He who the SON sets free is free indeed! I learned that being truthful is having freedom. Although the sexual trauma contributed to some of my rebellious and destructive behaviors; the power of God moved in this situation and forgiveness was my healing. I forgave my abuser. That's my truth!

Some have murdered, aborted, stolen, abused, manipulated, lied, denied, and accused. My advice would be to repent, confess your faults, and ask for forgiveness. Forgive yourself, forgive others and become free. It's all part of the *"Master's Plan."*

"O let the evil of the wicked come to an end, but establish the righteous; For the righteous God tries the hearts and minds."
Psalm 7:9NASB

Round 5

"A Pre-existing Cut of the Heart"

As a dating teenager, I looked at my boyfriend *that is now my husband*, as a cute, confident and courageous young man. He came from a stable, structured foundation. A two parent household which was inspiring to me. We met at the church house at the ages of fourteen and fifteen. I lost my virginity to him at the age of seventeen, and we gave birth to our first daughter in December of 1993. I disappointed so many, and felt every bit of it. Especially from some of the leaders in the church, as this was definitely frowned upon at the church house. I know I made a mistake, but can't help but wonder if those types of people have ever sinned, or is it that they just covered up their sin. For example, getting pregnant out of wedlock. Was it better to keep the baby and deal with their judgement, or get an abortion and move on with life like it never happened? Which choice would've been better?

Nevertheless I experienced my first church hurt at the age of seventeen. Forced to sit down with pastors, with no support from my household. I was spoken to like I was worthless. Like there was no grace for *me*. I later shared my experience with my grandmother, and she was livid that I was frowned upon. She asked my mom for clarity on why this took place. My mom's reply was that she was at work, and had no idea that things happened that way. Maybe it was miscommunication, but I was so hurt that I didn't want to return to church.

I was a young mother, married at twenty-two, second child at the age of twenty-four, and purchased our first home at the age of twenty-five. Anyone that is or has been married, knows that it requires work. When two individuals, that may have been raised differently, and have different views come together as one; there can be differences and conflicts. Looking back now, I realize that I focused more on the things that I liked and loved about him. Like when I would visit his family home, he cooked, cleaned, took out the trash, and his room always smelled good. He seemed to adore me, and he was smart, especially in mathematics. He also played an instrument in the school band. That was my type of guy. I believe a lot of these things were a reflection of the foundation set forth by his parents, which was a good thing. Out of all the things that impressed me, it was his interaction with his family and his mannerism that I admired the most. It wasn't long before I realized that I had given him credit for foundational behaviors, whereas that credit should've been given to his parents. For it was his parents that instilled that foundation. The foundation is always a great start, but when dating we must pay closer attention to the person's lifestyle in its entirety, and not just what we see on the surface level. A person's lifestyle is their truth. It tells you everything you need to know. Like who the person is, their habits, their likes, and dislikes. What makes them angry, and what makes them happy. How they deal with certain situations. We need to look at the entire picture and try not to focus so much on the preview. Not just what a person can do, but the real person on the inside. That is the core of a person, their true character. It is what you need to see when forming relationships. Especially when contemplating marriage.

When dating, it is important to know what type of person you are getting involved with. The good, that bad and the ugly. We not only need to look at the things that we enjoy about a person, but also at the areas that may need improvement. For example, lack of communication, bad habits, lack of affection, or bad attitudes. All things to consider before you make that vow before God. For me, there were a few things that had taken place during this time. We married very young, so of course we were both inexperienced, unprepared, and immature in some ways. As a minister, a wife, a mother, and a child of the Most High God. My intent has never been to reveal details to cause hurt or tear down anyone. Only to be transparent, so that I may help someone else. That transparency includes the personal issues I've struggled with also.

I was overly independent and although now married, I still handled situations on my own, as if I were single. I had a difficult time transitioning from my independent lifestyle, to a blended partnership with my husband. Most of my difficulties spilled over from my upbringing. I was perfectly fine with figuring things out on my own as I had done for so long, but now I had a partner. However, I continued to handle things independently. In doing this, I may have left him to feel as though I didn't need him. This only hurt me in the long run, because I deprived myself of help at times when I really needed it. I built a reputation of not needing his help, which led me to be overwhelmed in many situations while married.

One thing that caused a disconnect in our marriage, was his obsessive drinking. I became mentally exhausted, with having a partner that struggled with substance abuse. I wasn't prepared or trained on how to deal with this situation in my marriage. Honestly, I never realized while growing up that I would one day be someone's wife. That's one of the reasons why I believe mentorship is so important, and the reason that I am now a mentor for others. If I can help keep another couple from overlooking a smaller issue, that could possibly grow later on in the relationship or marriage; that would mean so much to me. It is important to deal with the difficult issues and conversations from the start. It can prepare you for a successful relationship and marriage from the beginning.

There was a point where I started to notice that the sexual trauma I endured as a child, had also affected my marriage. There were underlying emotions, that I hadn't fully dealt with. The way I communicated with my body language, or the times I became uncomfortable when I was awaken by my husband for intimacy. I would mentally revert back to my childhood and being awaken out of my sleep for sexual trauma. It took some time for me to realize what was happening to me, and how it was hindering my chances of success in my marriage. The cut in my heart was deep, and instead of going back to my corner to consult with my trainer *the Holy Spirit*, and have my coach *my Father God* to clean me up, I bled on my husband for so many years. As his struggle with alcohol abuse continued, I can only imagine that this may have given him a reason to indulge in it even more. It was a struggle to stay in the fight. There were days that I didn't want to see the ring or my opponent. I wanted to throw in the towel. What had we fallen in love with? What did he love about me back then? The days that he would look at me and often grin. What did I bring to the table back then, that I'm no longer capable of? What did he dislike about me, that he never uttered a word to me about, but perhaps told my friend? When considering marriage it's important to talk to your mate, and deal with the things you dislike head on. Talk about it and find ways to improve. Just as well as continuing to enjoy and highlight the things that you like. If you don't deal with the issues, problems, and concerns, they will linger; only to return at most often an even more difficult time. Set your demands and discuss your needs at the beginning. Be in tuned with your mate before the challenges arise. Marriage is not to be taken lightly. Find out everything you need to know about the person that you plan to spend the rest of your life with. If you don't it could potentially lead to major challenges when combined with life's demands and responsibilities such as children, finances, employment, etc.

In my opinion from twenty-three years of experience, I believe the key to a healthy marriage is good communication, and building together. If you're not communicating or building together it's hard to be on the same page, or know the needs of one another. Love is also a major key for any relationship or marriage. What happens when someone falls out of love? People can fall out of love, just as fast as they may have fallen in love. When the connection, and chemistry that you once shared dries up, or you allow resentment in your heart build up instead of the excitement that was once there. It could create distance. There have been times we both dropped the ball, and turned our attention toward other things. That's a big problem, because not only does your attention turn, but your affection for one another starts to diminish. Loss of affection can cause you to feel neglected and rejected; which was a familiar feeling that we both shared, but that can lead to strife.

Through my personal experience and counseling others, I have found that some people get married expecting one thing, but experience another and then are ready to quit. When you are not used to the pressure, it can be very uncomfortable. You bob and weave, but still get jabbed. Perhaps the challenges are deeper like verbal or physical abuse. Although no marriage is perfect-know the statistics of the one you're becoming one with, so you can rightfully accept or decline the fight. It's not an easy fix and for some it can be more difficult transitioning from single to married when you've been married to self for so long. The good can outweigh the bad, until the bad gets the best of you. What excited you at 15, no longer excites you at 30. Was it wrong to change for the better? We're not perfect, but we're not where we used to be. Growth may seem like a great thing when you see it in your spouse, but not such a great feeling when it's the actual thing that's pulling you all apart. How do you handle it when your spouse doesn't care for the woman or man that you've grown to become? What do you do when there are issues and one spouse would like to seek counsel and the other won't? What are some reasons you might be against counseling? What do you do when your spouse has lost respect for you? How can you rebuild trust in each other? Through the ups and downs, smiles and frowns I am grateful to God for keeping us both on our feet during this round. I once desired to be first in our marriage, but now I know better. *I pray that God will be first;* so that he can guide us from the *beginning* to the *end,* and show us *how* and *when* until the end.

"Hatred stirs up strife, but love covers all offenses"
Proverbs 10:12ESV

Round 6

"The Power of Darkness"

The power of darkness hovered over me for many years. This power included: Discouragement, Disappointment, Distress, Distraction, Devastation, Dilution, Demolition, Despair, and Destitution. All were leading to the path of DEATH! That demon led me to suicidal thoughts and attempts. It desperately wanted me to destroy the greatness of God that was within me. Even as a child, I would write letters as if I were saying goodbye to family and friends forever. I would withdraw from social contacts, and change my normal routines. Including eating, sleeping, and communicating. All these were signs of darkness. There is power in darkness, and we can't be naïve of the source from which it comes. We have to be aware of Satan's devices. It was so dark, that I couldn't see my opponent when it came time to fight. The clock was winding down. I thought to myself, what have I been doing all of this time? What have I done with the foundation I've received from age nine up until this point in my life? What accomplishments have I made thus far? With feelings of sadness and depression, I questioned my foundation and my growth.

I was nine years old when the sexual trauma started, and also when I received Jesus as my Lord and savior. This period of my life was significant for me, because it's also when I received the gift of the Holy Spirit, and speaking in other tongues *the heavenly language.* I started learning all about faith in God. I remember going to children's church wanting help, and wanting to become a better person. I just wanted more. As I listened to the ministers, speak about God. I remember the strong desire within me, to know this God that they spoke of. I wanted to know him on the same level that they did. Speaking with the ministers, caused me to desire God even more. With excitement I went up to the front when they called for altar call and I cried out to God. My tongue started making this sound that I didn't understand, and I felt something that I never knew I could feel. It was definitely a spiritual experience. Yet still after receiving the gift of the Holy Spirit, this didn't stop the power of darkness from trying to take me out. I would say it became more persistent. The cloud of darkness had a job, and that was to consume the light that was within me. It was my junior year in school when we moved back into the same bondage situation. The sexual trauma started back up again. As a way to end my torment, I took a bottle of pills, in an attempt of suicide-But God!

As I continued through life. In 2011, the spirit of darkness and suicide continued to hover over me. After a series of life events and losing my job of twelve years, I contemplated suicide again. As my husband left for work, I took my youngest daughter to school. My oldest daughter was residing in North Carolina during this time, and life had gotten so overwhelming for me. I had written out my suicide letter, and began to put my affairs in order. I had become weary to the point where I felt that I wanted to give up on life. I remember thinking to myself, "I must've been playing church, all these years," because I just didn't have the strength, will, or desire to continue this fight. How could I spend so much time in church, and still not have any strength or the desire to live? How will I make it to the next round without my strength? At that moment the telephone rung. It was just enough time for me to catch my breath. On the other end of the phone was my former supervisor Tarlouh. *(God always has a ram in the bush).* I hadn't spoken to her in a while. She asked how I was doing, and for the first time in a long time I was honest. I explained to her that I wasn't well. That I felt like a failure in my marriage, and with my children. I spoke about lack of money and being unable to find a job. I told her that I didn't feel smart, and I felt unworthy, because I could no longer contribute financially to my household. Things just weren't good for me.

She asked if I had read the book "The Battlefield of the Mind" by Joyce Meyer and I said no. I watched her on television and loved her messages, but I had never read her book. She ordered the book for me, and assured me that the book would arrive the next day. Instantly my thoughts changed from negative to positive. She had planted a word of encouragement, and I received and believed it. I always knew her to be a woman of her word. I had worked and been under her supervision for over 10 years. I know this encounter was designed by God; it was in the *"Master's Plan."* In that very moment my plans had changed from death to life, due to the power of someone else's tongue that was full of encouragement. I was full of excitement, as I waited in anticipation for the book of inspiration that was now on its way. It was as if *hope* jumped in me, and stirred up my faith. When I began to read the book, it was like a breath of fresh air. Each time I read and turned the page, I felt like I received new air and inspiration. It was an amazing feeling. I'm forever grateful to God, my former supervisor Tarlouh, and Joyce Meyer for that day. That book changed my life. My perspective changed on life issues, and I learned to be careful not to magnify the issues at hand. Problems will always be a part of life's journey, but we have a problem solver. I had to repent, start fresh and get back in the ring. Sometimes we can be in the ring fighting for so long, that our vision becomes cloudy. We are unable to clearly see our opponent. It's also possible to become delusional and mistake the ones in our corner for our enemies or vice versa. Then we miss the opportunities to knock the real enemy out.

The cares of the world can get the best of us, if we allow them to. Life can seem hopeless, but things aren't always as they seem. We must be focused, teachable, trained, equipped, rested, and ready for the fight. We have to be ready and able to respond to what may come next. In life, we will get hit with some hard blows, but we have power in our jabs and uppercuts. We draw that power through the word of God. I had to learn to wear my full armor of protection, especially during difficult times. To keep my eyes on my opponent at all times, and to make my next move my best move. After completing the book "The Battlefield of the Mind" by Joyce Meyer, I cried out to the Lord. "Precious Lord take my hand, lead me on, let me stand." Even though I might've been tired or weak, I didn't speak it. Instead, I asked that the light within me be illuminated to remove all the darkness that was trying to consume me. I was still standing at the end of this round. I fought through the discouragement, and discovered that I too am an encourager.

Suicide is never the will of God for our lives. Just as I mentioned in the beginning of this book, he has a purpose and a plan just for us. If suicidal thoughts try to overtake us, we can't sit in silence. We must reach out for help. Put a plan together, God has made a way for our escape. Pray, praise, worship and quote the Word of God out loud. These have been my spiritual weapons. Suicide Hotline 1-800-SUICIDE (784-2433).

"You have turned for me my mourning into dancing; you have loosed my sackcloth and clothed me with gladness"
Psalm 30:1ESV

Round 7

"The Battle of Restoration" The Greatest of all Times!

Sometimes in life we feel like things can't get any worse, but believe me it really can. I know some people who have gone through far worse things than I have. We all have different trials and tribulations that we must face. For me, I had to change my mindset and renew my mind almost daily to be restored. We must keep believing, moving and trusting. Don't stop. Don't become stagnant in the midst of battle. I know it's easier said than done. I have felt the same way many times, but I also know from my experiences that God is a God of restoration.

For example, after working for a great company for twelve years, the company went through reorganization and I was laid off. I had never experienced anything like this, but I took a deep breath and tried to focus on the next thing. I knew God wasn't surprised by this and I wasn't totally shocked either. I had a prayer life and heard God trying to prepare me for a move. Decisions had to be made, and some were bittersweet. We lived in Montgomery County Maryland during this time, and we loved it. It was the first home that we had purchased. I never thought I would move with my sister, but here we were renting our house and looking forward to our next steps. I personally went through a lot in 2010-2012, but as I look back God was ordering my steps. It was his plan, not mine, and Satan had a plan as well. We moved back to Prince Georges County where we lived with my sister Nicole, who is definitely my keeper. I realized that we needed each other. Although I didn't have a job for over a year while living there, I received severance pay. When money started getting low, I started losing control. The suicidal thoughts started creeping into my mind again. One day I sat at home alone, searching for a job, but nothing had come through. I received a call from my Aunt Veronica. During our conversation, she asked me about my spiritual gifts. I believe this conversation was destined by God. It led me to her church where I took several religious courses such as discipleship, growing God's family, finances etc. God was preparing me for the next BIG thing in my life. In 2012 I was trained then later ordained as a minister. Shortly after, I became a licensed business owner of Children of Destined Beginnings, my learning center. Where I teach children biblical principles. God had restored my mental state, then he restored my livelihood. He restored my finances, my job, and my relationship with my sister. These were all moves ordained by God. Although I was dealing with depression, almost all of my family lived close by. There was always someone around or not too far away. They held me accountable as I continued to punch my way through.

Prior to moving, I had lost friendships over misunderstandings and miscommunications. It was such a disappointment, but I realized that some relationships are worth fighting for. I had to be the bigger person, humble myself and apologize for the role I played in the miscommunication and wrong doing if any. I asked for God's will to be done in those moments. I knew that all relationships would not be saved, but reconciliation is necessary if we have a heart for God's people. Some things we will never learn, if we don't embrace constructive criticism. I personally found out that everyone we come in contact with has a purpose in our life. For some, their presence alone is so significant that you know it is designed by God. For others, their behaviors, or purpose may be to cause frustration, steal, kill, or destroy your life; or your purpose in life. We must spend time with the father, to determine the purpose of people so that we don't walk in deceit and entertain the assassin.

Needless to say after scoring so low in the last round, I needed a comeback, but I couldn't continue the fight without being restored. I went into the corner and consulted with my trainer *the Holy Spirit*, and my coach *my father God*. The one who created me, and the one that I trusted to put me back into this round to reestablish me. Whenever God restores something, he restores it to a place greater than it was before! I'm a living witness. I recall being in a church service, and a woman of God spoke on curses in our lives. I remember that Sunday like it was yesterday. I had invited my sisters to church, and to my surprise they were all available and attended with me. I had on a royal blue dress that day. I asked my sister Nikki to accompany me to the altar, as I felt the word that was preached spoke directly to our family and my spirit. As the first born child, I had a responsibility.

I went up to the altar for prayer, and the woman of God spoke a word into my life that I will never forget. She looked at me and asked if I was the eldest of my siblings. I nodded yes. The woman of God told me that "Satan had sifted my JOY like wheat." She said "you are operating, but without any JOY." It was so true. I was Missy, a wife to my husband, mother to my two girls, a daughter to my parents, a sister to my siblings, a business woman to my colleagues, and a friend to many, but something big was missing. My joy. Without joy I didn't have the full capacity of strength from the Lord. It was a spiritual attack. My joy had been stolen, and my strength was weakened. I was living day by day, lacking joy and strength. I became spiritually malnourished. Not realizing that God could not only be my strength in my weakness, but he could also fully restore me to the person he called me to be.

The woman of God prayed for me and touched me, then the power of God fell upon me. I slithered to the floor screaming as if I were possessed! Coughing up whatever was residing in me, which was a spirit of dilution. When I got up off the floor it was as if a burden had fallen off my shoulder, and chains were unlocked. I will never forget the deliverance that I received on that day. For a minute, I looked at the faces in the crowd and almost felt ashamed, but I realized I'd been set free. I would not be embarrassed of my freedom in that moment. Who the son of God sets free, is free indeed. God set that encounter up just for me. We have to go in the house of the Lord, expecting the move of God. He will provide, and we must make the sacrifice. Sometimes the sacrifice is simply getting where he needs you to be for a particular time. I might have been surprised at what took place, but God surely wasn't. I often think, if I wouldn't have attended service that day, I would have missed the message delivered through the preacher. If I was distracted, or not in tuned with the spirit of the Lord; I wouldn't have been compelled to walk to the altar. If I hadn't invited my sisters, their faith wouldn't have been strengthened. For we know faith comes by hearing, and hearing by the word of God. Had I been disobedient, I would have missed the opportunity to have my sister Nicole by my side as a witness and support. If I made the decision to stay in my seat and not accept the prayer, I wouldn't have received my deliverance from sadness. Satan used sadness and disappointments to steal my JOY! We must be aware of his devices.

God does things intentional. It was destined for this to take place, so that I could become a better person for myself, and all those that look to me for help. I'm nothing without my father God, the creator of all life. Who am I to act as if I have it all together, when truly I don't! My sister's look up to me. I need them to know that I've only made it thus far, due to the grace and mercy of God. We all get blessed when I carry and cover them in my prayers. I realized that I am the fighter in this ring, but the heavyweight title isn't just for me; but for my coach *my father God.* It all belongs to him. He has great plans. Not just for me, but for my sisters as well. In life, our roles or titles may change. It was part of his plan for me to go from fighter to trainer. So that with his power, I may help other fighters overcome their battles. I can't take God's glory, that would be a sin. He's the one who uses me to give, to grace and to be the guarantee. I know this because of his love for me. From the beginning, before we were born he announced some things over our lives. When spending time in his word, and being in fellowship with him I know my gifts, and those gifts are to be used for his purpose only. Not to be boastful, prideful, or un-useful. The word of God tells us that all good gifts come from above. Furthermore, it tells us that a man's gift makes room for him, and brings him before great men. It's so much revelation in this word alone.

I believe that this book will be before some great men and women that may not even know how much they've helped me along my journey. Then eventually it will become a play and even a movie, as it has been prophesied several times in my life. I'm ready for manifestation. There's no need to want to be someone else, and no need to be somewhere that you're not needed. No need of showing off what you can do, because the same God that blessed you with your gift has blessed someone else with a gift also. He has total control. I've been sitting on this book long enough and God said time is up! For those who deal with procrastination or fear; never let fear keep you from writing your story. If we don't be obedient and act swiftly on what God tells us to do, he may have someone else to do it. We must be obedient because if we don't it's a sin. When we hear or see the word sin, we often think of murder, adultery, or fornicating. Sin can simply be us trying to be in control of our lives, and the lives of other people. We have to deny ourselves, and know that our lives aren't our own. If that were so, then we could possibly control everything in it; and there wouldn't be a need for living by faith or trusting God at his word. Stay appreciative of what you're blessed with as if it were the first day you received it. Don't allow too much space between you and God. That would cause separation. A day may come when it's too late to be restored.

"Though you have made me see troubles, many and bitter, you will restore my life again; from the depths of the earth you will again bring me up."
Psalm 71:20NIV

Round 8

"Spiritual Conditioning"

The cave season - A season of the unfamiliar; isolation.
The fight to stand even if it means to stand alone. It's the
endurance of something difficult and uncomfortable without
complaint. When reflecting on my "cave season" I remember that
this was a challenging round for me. As my trainer *the Holy Spirit*
pulled me aside to solitude, he set me apart. It was different, I was
isolated, but not by choice. I was led to step down from ministry in
the four walls of my church, and took on church without walls.
Which consisted of family, friends, and strangers. At times I felt
alone. It was bittersweet for me, but I heard the voice of the Lord
and was led to move. Funny thing about it, the months prior to me
stepping down from ministry; I kept feeling like I was being led to
relocate to another state. Then I realized, that it wasn't a physical
relocation, but spiritual relocation.

My prayer has always been "Lord don't let me get lost in
ministry, in church or in the pulpit, but let me always hear you and
serve you." I never want to become arrogant or to give God's glory
to anyone but him. We have to be careful not to glorify ourselves,
making a name for self, or even making our mission greater than
the *"Master's Plan."* It's about him and the souls that he has
designed for us to win. I'm sure some didn't understand why I had
made the decision to step down. I'm not sure that I fully
understood what was happening either, and maybe I didn't know
how to articulate my actions. I didn't understand what was taking
place in the spiritual realm, but in the natural my grandmother was
ill. My oldest daughter was expecting a child and had become very
sickly, and my marriage was suffering and needed my attention.
Needless to say I had some work to do, and God was showing me
what and just how to do it. God knows what he can entrust to me.
Not just to do things out of routine or obligation, but to do what he

has called me to do. Not that I wasn't passionate about working in the church for his people, because we need laborers inside the church just as the Levites operated. I called on God and asked that his will be done, and to lead me to help the people that he wants me to help. I prayed for a fresh wind in the new direction he was leading me to. When I spoke with the referee *my overseer*, It was difficult to explain that my position had changed in ministry. I could only hope that one day our coach would make room for restoration, and dispute the disconnection, in his timing. I had to answer the call of God. Not just to have the title of minister, but to minister to all.

I had been in the cave for five months. Sometimes isolation can feel like you're infected with a contagious disease. I was in a place of waiting. Feeling a little unsure at times, even at the point of wavering. Solitude is one of the most important disciplines for spiritual life. Especially for leaders, and those who've accepted a high calling of God. One of the benefits of solitude is being released, and restored from the stress of ministry. God really restores our souls. He wipes the sweat from our brows, and he allows us to drink from his cup. He refills us, tightens our boxing gloves, and put us back into the ring with our teacher and trainer *the Holy Spirit*.

I attended a women's gathering, and the speaker was giving a word of encouragement. I knew God was going to speak to me, as I was led to be there. I went with great expectation, expecting to hear from God. While waiting for the service to begin, someone made disturbing remarks toward me that shook me to my core. The enemy is always busy. For a minute, I wanted to leave. I shed a few tears, stood up, walked to the front door, took a deep breath and got myself together. I changed my disposition, and continued to wait on the speaker. In that moment, I had to remind myself of why I was there. It was to receive the word from the Lord. Finally the speaker walked near me, and it was as if my heart was about to jump out of my chest. It was beating so fast that I felt as though it had skipped a beat. My coach was about to openly speak to me, and I was ready to hear and do, but I was also looking for confirmation! She looks over to me and says "Woman of God, never stop praying because your prayers reach a part of heaven that most people can't reach! No matter what season you're in never stop praying." Prayer is direct communication with the coach *my Father God*. She continued, "You've been in a cave season, but when you come out of this, you will walk with more power and authority like never before!" What a comeback. I jumped around that ring and yelled, I will win! I felt the crowds energy. There was chatter, and cheering. Some that used to cheer for me, now was chatting against me. Some who promoted me, now shunned me, but I remained focused on the words my coach had just spoken to me. At one point, I closed my eyes, while jumping around. With my eyes closed, I couldn't tell who was for me or who was against me. It didn't matter, because God allowed the cheering to be louder than the chatter. What most people didn't know and couldn't hear was my coach *my father God* telling my trainer *the Holy Spirit* "keep her back stable and her knees from being feeble." The tears flowed from my eyes as living water.

It wasn't just the physical people that were there in the natural, but it was the demonic forces that were there in spirit. I received my confirmation that I had no reason to feel ashamed or embarrassed, for I wasn't put away; but God had me hidden in the cave for his purpose. Sometimes isolation is a good thing, being set apart for God's purpose is necessary. Due to the many distractions and temptations in our daily lives that can be overwhelming and can deter us from his plan for our lives. During this time I was away from others, the dreams, visions and the word helped me to stay grounded and gave me insight on where God was taking me.

"Be still and know I am God." (Psalm 46:10)

This was confirmation that my coach and trainer *(my Father God, and the Holy Spirit)* were both working together for my good. I hadn't spoken to anyone about the pain that I had been experiencing in my knees, joints and back, due to being knocked around in a previous round. I didn't want my friends, or opponent *(the enemy)* to identify my weakness. Receiving those words of confirmation indicated that God knows everything about us, even if we never utter it out of our mouths. He knows our every need. Intellectual, physical, and emotional. He cares about our cares. The coach of our lives is very much in tuned to not only whom he has called us to be, but what we will go through and how we will come out. It's important to give GLORY to the one and only that sees us through our trials. We tell God the glory belongs to him, and we give him the glory, but we must be careful that our actions are also in alignment. The glory of God is more than what we could ever imagine. It's not just a saying, but it's majesty.

God took me into the spiritual realm and allowed me to see souls that I will reach for his glory. Early one morning, before the Royalty Worship Experience conference I had a spiritual encounter with God. During this encounter, my spirit left my body and went into the clouds and I was in the heavenly realm, where I only saw babies and angels. I heard a voice say "heaven rejoices over one soul," and then the angel's mouth opened wide. What a wonderful sight and feeling it was to be in the actual presence, and glory of God. I trembled, yet hearkened, in the presence of his Glory, that I could barely contain to be there long. It was the most powerful thing I'd ever experienced. It prepared and renewed my mind for the next round of winning souls. I prayed that the same glory that he allowed me to experience, would fall on the souls that would come to the first Royalty conference; and he absolutely answered my prayers. The scene was set, the team was ready, the people came in and I the fighter was anointed and steady. The anointing and the Glory was so heavy, people were delivered and their old ways had to die. I screamed FIRE! The altar was formed before the service even began. People were touched and even changed before we began to sing. He sent the captives to be set free. Those who felt hopeless, unworthy, depressed and full of anxiety. The residue of me being in his glory shifted the atmosphere. His glory demanded the attention of the crowd. I was fearless in this round. I was reminded by my dear cousin Latonya right before this round started, not to be focused on the empty seats, but reaching the souls that filled the seats. I reflected again on the voice from my encounter that said "Heaven rejoices over one soul." Some were there for support, some were there for deliverance, but the spirit of God told me that everyone that showed up and was ready to receive would experience his glory. The encounters and visions get greater and greater, and I am thankful to God for using me as his vessel.

"Where there is no vision, the people are unrestrained, But happy
is he who keeps the law."
Proverbs 29:18NASB

Round 9

"Accepting the Call"

Obedience has been a big part of accepting the call of God. It's the act of following instructions, complying with rules, and submitting to authority. At times we may feel or believe we can make our own way, but we can't. Truthfully, when I walked in disobedience I was noncompliant with authority; which always led me to sacrificing something. I am a loving parent and I instruct, or advise my children to do things at times. If they choose not to obey, they will soon find out that there are consequences to face, which is the direct result of disobedience. When we walk in disobedience we take the risk of losing more than we gain. You get temporary satisfaction, but the consequence and what you lose holds more value. With my daughters, I call this my 3LT's (3 lose T's), which are three things that we personally lose when we don't adhere to instructions.

1. Time - A limited period for action to take place. (Timely manner) We waste time when we are not walking in obedience.
2. Trust - Confidence and care in someone who's honorable. (confidant) The person who gave the instruction may lose confidence in you to make the right decisions.
3. Tenacity - The ability to stick firmly to a plan without doubting. (determination) Having tenacity shows discipline. When you lose tenacity, you lose your credibility of being reliable.

Sometimes being obedient can be challenging, but it's necessary to get through a situation *sooner* rather than *later*. Have you ever noticed that we may endure a situation longer than we have to, because we did something without heeding to wisdom? That situation that you kept going through over and over because you didn't gain wisdom from it the first time around.

*For example: It could've been something as simple as purchasing furniture through a company on a 90-day credit with the intent to pay it off quickly. The purchase may not have been a priority at the time, and you may have even heard the Holy Spirit tell you not to make the purchase. However, you go against that feeling in the pit of your stomach. Through your disobedience you make the purchase anyway, with the intent to pay it off within three months. Then life happens, and now you're unable to fulfill that financial obligation; so you end up paying double or triple the amount for something that now doesn't seem worth it at all. A possible consequence for disobedience. Or perhaps you and your family have big plans to excel. You all **meet** occasionally to **strategize** and to **confirm** that everyone is on the same page, only to find out that one of the family members has difficulty with being **persistent** and has chosen to go off in the opposite direction. Unable to **stand firmly** to the plan agreed upon due to doubting and wavering, and now losing the connection and the **fight** to retain the **goal**. Time is wasted, trust is broken, and the tenacity is now lost. The 3LT's are all valuable in life.*

Disobedience is rebellion and stubbornness is a sin. It involves far more than being independent and strong minded. The scripture equates the two with witchcraft and idolatry. Therefore, just as the word of God says in II Corinthians 10:5 we must cast down arguments and every high thing that exalts itself against the knowledge of God, bringing every thought into captivity to the obedience to Christ. What this means is when we have thoughts contrary to the word of God, we must first consciously submit to God, and not our imagination. Secondly, cast the imagination away; throw it with force! I am who I am today because of both obedience and disobedience. Although God forgives us from our mistakes, I am aware that we still deal with consequences. On the other hand I've learned through my own children that if we don't allow room for mistakes, we miss the opportunity for growth. Can God use our mistakes and turn them around for our good? Yes indeed! I'm not saying that our sacrifice isn't important, but rather we should look at the reason we had to sacrifice in the first place. When I think about my personal disobedience, I think about the disappointment I have caused God. Once we know we've sinned, we should seek forgiveness by repentance; so that our relationship may be restored with God. I thank God that he still loves me and continues to use me despite my faults. I've learned that my relationship with God is far more important than anything else. Yes, he is the God of many chances, but let us learn and obtain knowledge from Saul's mistake in the book of 1Samuel chapter 15. Saul's Kingdom was taken away due to his disobedience. We must act responsibly with what God has entrusted to us. Whether it's your marriage, ministry, or millions. After recognizing my error and spending significant alone time with God, I had an ear to hear and eyes to see. I had spiritual encounters with him that are hard to describe, yet my heart longed for more encounters. Although my mind couldn't always fathom what was taking place, my spirit welcomed these encounters; but sometimes I was afraid of what I would experience.

One encounter started off as a dream, but turned into an open vision. I was with a child, and we went up to the clouds. It was the presence of God that took us into the clouds where it was angelic. I saw one angel in the **center** of the clouds. Perhaps it was my assigned angel. This was a huge church with empty pews. My eyes looked at the first two rows, and thought I would be seated there, but I was placed in the **center** of a platform. It was a beautiful purple and gold ambiance, and I started to pray with such a graceful anointing. Then suddenly, I went from there to being flown into the **center** of two concrete walls. I kept bouncing between two walls. I was confused. I remember thinking "what am I doing here?" After reviewing this encounter, being in the **center** caused me to stick out. I started to study the word "center."
Center: The point that is the focus of attention, a place area or group of people exerting influence. We can be the center of a lot of things.

When I returned from this open vision, I was asked these questions "will you chose to be the center of *man (self)* or *godliness (holiness)?*" "Will you seek to please *Man* or *God*?" I realized that through that vision, God was showing me where he intended for me to be. However, if I didn't adhere to *his* way and allowed my feelings, emotions, people or fear to grip me, it would be just like my vision. I would bounce between two concrete walls with no way of getting where I should've and could've been.

Sometimes when we go through hurtful experiences, it tests our faith and character. I had gone through, and I wanted to be done with religion. Honestly, hurt is experienced everywhere, not just in the church. It is experienced at all types of places, on your job, in church, in public places and even in your own home. Hurt happens, and it comes from all types of people that we encounter. I am sure that we have all caused hurt at some point in life. Repent, forgive and move forward. I had to remember that my life isn't my own. I belong to God, and he has a plan for me. It shall come to pass. So I wiped those tears and had to affirm boldly that God is my creator. God is love and God is in control. He is my joy and my peace. He has shown me his promises for my life. I can choose to accept it or not, but he has shown the results and the expected end. For that I'm forever grateful. I would be lost without, the visions, dreams and encounters from the Lord. He's our creator, so he absolutely knows what each one of us needs for this journey we're on because it's all for his glory. I understand fully, that my preaching, encouraging, and soul winning is all a part of his plan. He uses us to do his work on earth, but he's not limited to just using us. It's a privilege to serve and to be used by God. We ask God to use us, but we want to tell him how, or what we're done with, when he's already designed the how. He just wants us to hear and do. Submission is better than offering, just as obedience is better than sacrifice.

"To do righteousness and justice is desired by the LORD more than sacrifice."
Proverbs 21:3NASB

Round 10

"Fighting With God's Authority"

The cave season is over and I have gone through the fire. I've chosen to be obedient and I'm walking with more power, resilience and authority than I ever have before. I'm fighting to win souls. Souls that need to come out of darkness into the light, out of religion into relationship, out of repetitive behavior into experience, and out of service to encounters with our father God. The most enlightening thing I've learned about this whole experience and fighting this fight, is that this fight is not just for me. This fight is also for the people who look to me for guidance, wisdom, and understanding of the word of God. There have been times when I've felt that people depended on my power punches. Not just for me to swing them, but to actually land the punches. I deliver the punches through the power and might of God.

I'm called to preach, I will open the bible to preach and teach the Gospel of Christ, not my opinion. I will respect the word of God and study to show myself approved. God gave me the idea and strength to start a mentorship program "Royalty" which is a deliverance ministry. Which scripture reference is: **1 Peter 2:9 "But you are a chosen people, a royal priesthood, a holy nation, God's special possession, that you may declare the praises of him who called you out of darkness into his wonderful light."** But the scripture before and after this verse is what really helped me understand it all. Verse 8 says, **"A stone that causes people to stumble and a rock that makes them fall." They stumble because they disobey the message-which is also what they were destined for.** Then after he tell us in verse 9 that we are chosen verse 10 tells us we once *were* **not** a people, but *are* **now** the people of God, who had not obtained mercy but now have obtained mercy. If we can remember this passage while going through there will be a stone (obstacle) that will cause us to stumble, but we have to look beyond where we are, and what we see. We must get to know God, so we can get to know what we're destined for. I'm so grateful to know what I'm created to do. It's not just to be someone's wife, mother, mentor and friend. I'm created, called and chosen to a higher calling; and that is to be a humble devoted servant of the Lord God. I must serve in all capacities of my life that has been given to me. I will take opportunities, and make accomplishments with the mercy God has granted. His mercy has helped me obtain forgiveness, favor, and friends for life. His mercy has helped me through correction, connections and counseling. His mercy has directed me thru prayer request, the countless hours of mentoring, and the approach of reaching and teaching souls. In this round, I learned the benefit of mercy! Unmerited favor is another word for mercy. God's mercy has opened doors of opportunity for me and I'm amazed each time. For I know that it's not about how much I know, or how fast I am, but simply how much God loves me.

"Do not remember the sins of my youth, nor my transgressions; according to Your mercy remember me, for Your goodness' sake, O LORD."
Psalms 25:7NKJV

Although my daughters are both grown, at the ages of twenty six and twenty. I led them both to Christ, so I continue to stand by them during their shaping, and molding process. Quite often people are led to Christ, but then later feel like there's no one to help guide them through life situations. There have been occasions when they've both come to me overwhelmed, afraid, or full of anxiety. I use the power and authority to rebuke and cast out fear! For God didn't give us a spirit of fear, but of LOVE, POWER and a SOUND MIND. It's amazing to be used by God, to be able to bring peace, healing, and deliverance to his people. For those who really know me, know that it's not in my own power, but its God working through me; so I give him all the glory and the honor. Even my immediate family members, who see my imperfections, but still notice the authority that I carry. I'm honored to be able to be that to my family, as they share me with so many people. I know at times they may just want me to themselves, but most times they are fine with sharing me. They understand what I'm called to do, and who I am called to. It makes me proud when they refer people to me for the sake of edifying, but what I appreciate most about my family is that most of them recognize the gift that I am. They respect and appreciate what they have in me and know it's not only for them, but for whomever God sees fit. For it didn't come from me, but from the spirit of God. Everyone has a gift, or gifts and we are to let our light shine. We may go through trying times and feel pressed on every side, but we are not down for the count. For example, balancing home, work, social, and ministry can be tough, but it surely can be done. Listening to the father in my prayer time has helped me regain focus when I get off balance. No one is perfect so we must depend on his guidance.

One afternoon I was driving to my daughter's college alone, it was approximately two and a half hours from home. I rode in silence expecting and anticipating hearing from God, and the words he spoke to me really encouraged and gave me more motivation to press in. He said "I created you to be powerful instead of pitiful." We must remember that there is only one you, so let's be the best YOU that you can be. We all have a course to run, so let's do it with the power and authority that God has given us without comparing ourselves to others. The Lord has made us unique and called us to do specific things while on earth. Remember to do things that matter, your reward will be in heaven. My blood sisters see the love and honor I give to my sisters in Christ, but I must not forget my blood line and the foundation and principals our mother taught us. To love each other no matter what. There are four of us and we are each other's keepers. When one falls down, one of us if not all, will lift her up. It's not strange that my mom had four girls. As we go through life, and the ups and downs. We will continue to smile, shine and support one another. I'm extremely happy that I was blessed with two daughters Tiara and Kaylah, in which I can teach them the same principals. I walk boldly as a child of God, with my head up high. Believing, praying, praising and worshiping the Lord. I am not ashamed of who I am and where I come from. Neither am I ashamed of the things I've been through, because It's made me the woman I am today. Some feel that I spoil, or do too much for my daughters. For me, it was important to have a balance. Not only so that my daughters never feel that I neglected them or put them last, but to make certain that I was a good steward over what God has entrusted me with. God gave them to their dad and I, for such a time and purpose as this. To love and train them. So often we use the scripture **Proverbs 22:6 "Train up a child in the way they should go and when they are old they will not depart,"** but we have to really look deeper into this scripture. I recently read this scripture again and received a fresh revelation. We shouldn't train them to be like us, or try to live their lives for them, but instead the word is implying that we ought to train our children to choose the right path. We as parents don't always get it right. I know I didn't, but now I ask God for help since he created them, and then loaned them to us to guide.

Round 11

"Losing a Round (Grandma)"

The grandmother I had was a superwoman, who never asked for help until her last days. She was a strong woman and I'm honored to be a part of her legacy. I called her "Ma," God saw fit that I gave her what she needed at the end. It was definitely in the *"Master's Plan."* I once received a word of prophesy over my life, that I was the Joseph of my family. I didn't quite understand the phrase until I read and saw the story of Joseph. God ensured me his word to be true: ***Jeremiah 1:5KJV*** **"Before I formed thee in the belly I knew thee; and before thou camest forth out the womb I sanctified thee, and I ordained thee a prophet unto the nations"**

In 2010 I had the first dream of her dying, I woke up shaking and crying because it felt so real. God saw fit that my husband was right beside me, when normally he would've already left for work. In the dream, the family was all in a hospital. I told the family that whoever went in to see her, must have her repent, confess, forgive and accept God. In the dream, I was passionate but adamant not knowing that I would be the one in real life with this assignment. Joseph was a dreamer, so I also received a clearer understanding of me being the Joseph of my family during the transitioning of my grandmother.

During my grandmother's last days, God told me to go see her for twenty-two days straight. No matter what, I had to do just that. When your teacher gives you an assignment, it must be completed or you will not receive a passing grade. During the twenty-two days, I was just to be there. I didn't have a special prayer or specific duty beforehand. I simply obeyed him. Some days I would just listen, some days I would pray, some days I would take her where she needed to go, but either way I was there… I was favored by my grandmother the late **Leslie E Da'Costa**. With favor came blessings. You have to be a blessing to receive true favor, and when you're favored you in return are the blessing. Although I felt like I lost this round, I actually won. I was obedient and went after my grandmother's soul, instead of fame. She once was lost, but now she's found. Souls are the most important thing to God, his words says he desires everyone to come into the knowledge of the truth. That included my grandmother.

In life, things are set up a certain way. We may not understand everything in the beginning or even in the end, but know that God has a plan and you're a part of it. My grandmother raised me. She favored me from the beginning of my life, to the end of her life. She had 6 children and I was like her 7th, she worked hard with two to three jobs at times. She had reached a placed in life where she and my grandfather accomplished purchasing a house together. The house wasn't just a house or home, it was a safe place to so many including my sisters and I. This superwoman wore many hats. She was so much to so many people. By spending time with her, I learned that she wore many without others even knowing she wore them. The load was heavy for sure, but God gave her strength to endure. Time after time people imposed, asked, took and she kept the hat of giving on her head until the day she departed from here. I often wonder, how she continued to give so much to so many without fainting. I've watched my grandmother my whole life with this big heart of hers, and I gained wisdom of what to do for my family. Her example also showed me what not to do with a big heart. Her life taught me something bigger. It taught me not only to fight for those I love, and those God assigned me to, but to fight for myself. It's necessary to remove the hats of heaviness at times. In this round while fighting my opponent I felt a bit prepared and powerful, but I know the power doesn't mean much if I don't land a punch. I might have been a little tired at times, but I didn't get discouraged. I heard my trainer in a small voice telling me not to drop my hands. She's resting from her labor, she's finished her fight here on earth, but I will continue to fight the good fight of faith. I've had a few more dreams of grandma since she left here, but just confirmation that she's no longer suffering. Sometimes we can selfishly want things so badly that our love ones suffer instead of resting. I'm thankful I'm in a better place mentally and spiritually.

When I think of how I planned, organized and eulogized my grandmother's funeral. It wasn't easy, but it was necessary. There is no way that I would've thought that I could do it, nor did I do it in my own might. I know it was God that chose and equipped me for the assignment of delivering my grandmother's eulogy. When going through this round, I didn't cut corners or cheat. I didn't have anyone else do what I knew that I was capable and chosen to do. I couldn't allow the opinion of others to dictate how I obtained, defended or achieved this win. It started with the mind. Although I could've bowed out gracefully before the funeral, I was reminded that I have the mind of Christ. That I can do all things through Christ Jesus who strengthens me, so I pressed on. When my grandmother became ill God gave me specific instructions and I knew he wouldn't bring me this far and not give anymore. It may be important for some to receive acknowledgement when they do something for others; but it's more important that we as people give back to the ones who we say we love, cherish and honor. I loved my grandmother, so I did this out of honor.

When I reflect on the loss of my grandmother it also causes me to reflect back on the year that my brother was murdered. It was one year before I lost my grandmother. My father called me from prison to tell me that his only son and my only brother had been shot and killed. This was devastating news, and I was in shock with how things happened. I felt helpless, but prayer and the support of Pastors, prayer warriors, and close friends that God used helped me through the difficult days that were ahead. In my pain, I still pressed and did what I was chosen to do. The image that I kept having of him lying and dying alone had disturbed me. I shared what happened to my brother with a friend, and a girl reached out to me and told me her friend was the paramedic that was with my brother when he died. She explained how they tried to revive him. It brought me so much comfort to know that someone possibly prayed, and tried to save his life. That he was not alone. I am so happy that my father and I were in a good place at this time, because we needed each other back then; and we surely need each other today. Every time we go to visit my mother together at the nursing facility, she lights up at the sound of his unique voice; and at the sight of my face. Her eyes speak to me and I tell her to "fight for her life."

RIP Grandma, Aunt Helen, Aunt Louise, Aunt Benita, Brother Davon and to my dear friend Keisa, and my Godfather Jerome (Snaggs). I sure wish that you were here to witness TFOML project, but I appreciate the time God allowed us to have with one another. Each of your roles in my life were destined and will never be forgotten.

Round 12

"The Enemy is Defeated"

In April 2019, I had a dream that someone I love and trusted told me that I had throat cancer. In May of 2019, I started to experience throat issues. In June of 2019, I had a biopsy done and the results were pre-cancerous. Now this could've been a very scary and unsure time for me. As my mom suffered 2 more major strokes on May 6th 2019, my father was in severe pain the same day! We were all in pain on Friday, May 3, 2019. I remember the day so clearly. I received a call that my niece walked into my mother's apartment to find her laying out on the living room floor, I thought My God! I had spoken to my mom the night before, about four times prior to going to bed. I thought it was strange that mommy and I talked for about 20 minutes, then we hung up and she called right back. We talked for another 10 minutes, and she did this about two more times. We laughed because it was if she had to tell me everything she was thinking right then and there…. I smiled and said ok mommy I love you. I could hear in her voice the adoration, as most often she would beat me to saying "I love you". That was the last time we actually had a conversation. The last time I heard her voice so clear and precise.

As I continued to reflect back on the dream I had in April, I'm thankful for God's guidance. In some of my prophetic dreams, I experienced spiritual warfare. I had to learn to discern the difference as sometimes they can seem similar since I'm in the spiritual realm, and don't understand everything. What I do know and understand now are the plans that God *has* for me vs. the plan that Satan *wants* for me. The encounters are pivotal. To see the side of the face of Jesus. His ear inkling to my prayers, to experience a burning fire that permeated my body inside. To see a brass ark on the alter between me and the spirit of God is definitely real, and no one can tell me differently. I don't know why God chose me, but I'm glad he did, and I desire to please him. I'm persecuted, but not forsaken, thanks be to God. I may have gotten pretty beaten up, and even knocked down in the last round but I won't lose the fight. Therefore I will not lose heart. 2Corinthians' 4:16 I became tired, and my troubles surrounded me. It almost shook me to the point of no return, but I'm thankful it didn't take me out for the count. Trouble is to be expected when in a fight. We must keep our guards up and stay off the ropes. My coach told me to believe that if I fall, that I will get back up. My trainer told me to believe that he will help me carry out the fight. No one told me that this would be an easy fight. Not my trainer, coach, teacher or supporters. I know my enemy wants this win, but I know God didn't bring me this far to leave me in the middle of this fight. I fight my battles with prayer, since it first starts with our thoughts; then from our thoughts to words, our words, become actions, from actions to habits, from habits to character, and from character to our DESTINY!

Lastly, the almighty God fights my battles. We may become anxious or discouraged when going through battles. We may even start to doubt God, but no matter the situation he is sovereign and cares about our cares. When I would become anxious and fearful, I would beat myself up for not believing that God would come through for me. On the other hand, when I fasted, prayed, and remained still, he showed up in the ring.

The LORD will fight for you; you need only to be still.

God allows trouble so we will remember to be humble and to recognize that the POWER is from him, not us. It's the power of GOD at work within us. The power of God that's saving us all who believe shall be saved. Just as the centurion spoke in Matthew 8:8 I am not worthy, that God should come under my roof: but I speak the word of God only and I will be healed.

Some miracles take 40 days,
My personal fast consisted of a few things. I had to guard my mind and not ponder on the negative thoughts of being sick. My thoughts, caused me to look up my symptoms after seeing the results and based on how I felt. Panicking and fearing the worse. I

started speaking what it could've possibly been. I felt defeated even before being diagnosed from a doctor. Once I went to the word of the Lord, I was able to get a hold of my thoughts, I then was able to rebuke, cast away and declare that I shall not die, but live to declare the works of the Lord.

Lions show their teeth because they believe it instills fear in the opponent, so when the enemy shows their teeth; stay still, and don't run. Look the enemy in the eye and plead the blood of Jesus with authority! Be Strong and Courageous. God trusts me to care for, pray for, and to intercede for his people; so that no one will be lost. For heaven rejoices over one soul. It's a responsibility that can't be taken lightly, as he already paid the cost of the fight! Anyone can fight, but I came to WIN.

Whether you go through the tunnel, the belly of the whale, the lion's den, or even the fire, you will come out victorious!

"I shall not die, BUT live and declare the works of the Lord."
Psalm 118:17

LATRICIA JACOBS

Photos

Missy and Mom (Cassandra)

Missy and her biological Father

56

Photos

Missy

Missy fighting to overcome

Photos

Missy ministering the word of God

Missy

Resources

National Suicide Prevention Lifeline
Call 800-273-TALK (8255)
- Trained counselors are available 24/7
- Information is private and confidential

Citations/Credits

All scripture quotations noted ESV are taken from THE ENGLISH STANDARD VERSION. Crossway Bibles. (2007). ESV: Study Bible: English Standard Version. Wheaton, III Crossway Bibles. Used by permission. All rights reserved.

All scripture quotations noted KJV are taken from THE KING JAMES VERSION. Dallas, TX: Brown Books Publishing. (2004). The Holy Bible: King James Version. Brown Books Publishing. Used by permission. All rights reserved.

All scripture quotations noted NKJV are taken from the NEW KING JAMES VERSION. Nashville: Thomas Nelson. (1982). Used by permission. All rights reserved.

All scripture quotations noted NASB are taken from the NEW AMERICAN STANDARD BIBLE. La Habra, CA: Foundation Publications, for the Lockman Foundation. (1971). Used by permission. All rights reserved.

All scripture quotations noted NLT are taken from the NEW LIVING TRANSLATION. Tyndale House Publishers. (2004). Holy Bible: New Living Translation. Wheaton, III: Tyndale House Publishers. Used by permission. All rights reserved.

Ruyter, D. (n.d.). *Dadtography.com*. Retrieved from https://www.dadtography.com/definition-of-dad-vs-father-and-a-fathers-right-to-parent/

Pearson. (n.d). *LDOCE Online*. Retrieved from LDOCE Online: https://www.ldoceonline.com/dictionary/abandon

Frank Outlaw Quotes. (n.d.). Retrieved from Goodreads: https://www.goodreads.com/quotes/6507450-watch-your-thoughts-they-become-words-watch-your-words-they

Testimonials

Minister Missy Jacobs has been a sister, friend, and mentor to me. Although we have known each other for years, it was recently when we reconnected that she impacted my life in a great way; for such a time as this. As a leader in Royalty Diadem, Minister Missy has pushed me beyond my limits, encouraging me to move forward in the things of God. I recall a time of her selflessly praying with me through one of the most challenging moments in my life. I know God used her on that day. This is just one of many testimonies I can share about my sister, friend and mentor Minister Missy Jacobs.

I have watched Minister Missy push past her own challenges while continuing to serve others. I am a witness to how God consistently uses her to touch the lives of many. Minister Missy Jacobs is a wife, mother, sister, daughter, friend, warrior, a true woman of God who is also a prayer warrior and servant of the Lord with a heart for God's people.

-Tamika "TJ" Woodard

Missy's purpose to foster the healing of the broken-hearted is directly from God and I'm a witness to an amazing ministry that God has placed in her. During a critical time when I was mentally at the lowest point in my life The Holy Spirit prompted me to reach out to Missy for Spiritual guidance. I had no clue what God had in store for me. Missy immediately through God's guidance, breathed God's living water into me! She did not stop until his word was fully received and engraved in my heart. My transformation is a true testimony of God's undeniable love for me! Something I had never felt until my first session with Missy. There is no question that Missy and her ministry Royalty is God sent. I have seen lives changed in the Royalty sessions. Thanks to my encounter with Missy, I'm now a Royalty leader and also actively pursuing the purpose that God has placed in my heart. I am so thankful that she didn't give up on her God given mission to heal the broken-hearted.

-Sherrita

Missy has been my friend for many years. I've watched her along this journey and I'm so proud of her growth and obedience. I joke that she has a phone directly connected to God. We've been through a lot together and supported each other through a lot. I'm grateful she was there. I chose her as my daughter Cheyenne's Godmother on purpose. Not only was she my best friend but I saw what an amazing mother and wife she was. I knew if something happened to me, she would take good care of her, provide a strong foundation and help her become the great woman of God she was preordained to be!

Royalty has offered a great platform for so many to find peace and help heal their emotional wounds. I feel blessed to have been a part of it. It helped me to peel back layers and start to know my gifts and grow spiritually. There is more growing to be done but I'm thankful that Royalty helped launch that within me.

-Jennifer R. Phillips

I've known Missy since we were students at the same elementary school. She created a cheerleading group that practiced during recess. I remember wanting so badly to be a part of the team. The group was precise, uniform, and committed. I watched Missy direct us, help us, learn routines, and encourage us to be great. Even in elementary school, she was a leader. She was focused, supportive, encouraging, determined, and caring. When I joined the team, I was shy, but Missy encouraged me, and I became confident in my ability and my place on her team. Fast forward to present day, and Missy, once again, positively impacted my life. I attended the Royalty Diadem Conference and experienced the presence of God. Once again, I wanted to be a part of Missy's vision. But I felt like I didn't belong. I had stopped attending church, and I felt like I was so far outside of God's will, that I was afraid to ask her about joining. One year later, in 2018, I was in a horrible place mentally. I was suicidal, and I wanted to give up. I called Missy and she stopped everything that she was doing to see about me. She asked where I was, and came to me. She sat with me, and she talked to me for hours in the parking lot. Missy was encouraging, she assured me of God's love for me, but most importantly, she showed me God's love. She consistently checked on me, prayed for me, and with me. She made sure that suicidal spirit was gone. In one of the most difficult weeks of my life, God showed me how much he loves by sending Missy to me to intervene on my life, and I have not been suicidal since. Missy is the example of God's love that we can see, feel, and touch. She is God's disciple, and she has a heart for God's people. Her ministry has touched me, and so many others, and I thank God for her. I am blessed to call her friend.

-Sherletta Barrow

I have known Minister Missy since she was in her mother's womb! I have not been with her through every experience in her life, but I know that each of them have been to develop her for the times we are living in. For this generation and many to come. She is an effective and powerful weapon for the Kingdom of God. She walks by faith, and embraces the the power and authority that Jesus commands her to stand in. I praise God for her life!

-Minister LaTonya

I was broken, hurt, abused and ready to give up on life! I've been ostracized most of my life; labeled wild and crazy, but really I'm just misunderstood. God placed my sister in my life to rebuild me, encourage me, strengthen me, love me and resuscitate me. She puts herself aside and speaks directly to your need; so that you can be healed, delivered and set FREE!

-Shakia

Royalty has been a great outlet for myself and my children. Through Royalty I've learned a lot about life, and gained the understanding that we will go through things; but keep God first and he will lead you in the right direction. I've shared stories about my life, my trials and tribulations with no judgement; but love, understanding and excellent feedback. I enjoy every meeting that we have attended. I wish they were longer. I met Missy when I was going through a terrible time in my life realistically and spiritually (middle of the valley) and I lost myself; spiritually, mentally and emotionally. Missy immediately jumped in with open arms, an open heart, and listening ears to be there for me. I've cried rivers to her, and she never turned me away; but met me halfway. She has become a sister to me, and I love her for having my back. I suffered mentally (felt like I was going crazy due to major panic attacks and anxiety attacks) and spiritually (questioned God for things he allowed to happen to me) but I forever will remember what Missy said to me in one of our Royalty meetings. She said "why not you Edol?" Since that day, I say that to myself when I start to question God. I love God, and I know God loves me, because with all the hardship I've experienced in life to this day, I'm still standing strong. I still believe, and he has blessed me with three humble, intelligent, God fearing children. I thank God every day for them!

-Edol

Minister Missy Jacobs, is my bloodline Cousin. I had no idea that the Lord was going to orchestrate; Minister Missy to lead me to my purpose. She is beyond a powerful woman of Great Influence! She seeks God on every area, she listens and waits for His instructions, and then activates the Word of God's Truth. Minister Missy's vision for Community Care could only be spirit led. To sit under and follow her leadership is such a honor to me! Minister Missy has pushed me to levels that I couldn't even imagine I could or would go too. I am extremely blessed to be part of Royalty Diadem; under the leadership of Minister Missy Jacobs.
This ministry truly stands on the word of God.

2 Corinthians 6: 3-10
-Nicole "Nikki" Jones

ABOUT THE AUTHOR

Latricia "Lady M" Jacobs was born in Washington, DC. She is a devoted wife, and mother. Minister Latricia M. Jacobs, known to many as "Missy" is an awesome woman of God. She is a devoted servant of the Lord; gifted with dreams and visions to evangelize, reach the lost, and win souls for the kingdom. Her character exemplifies integrity, coupled with a tenacity that captures the hearts of all who yearn to be delivered.

Missy was born, raised and educated in the Washington, D.C. Metropolitan area; it is here, that the foundation was set. In 1981, Missy's parents joined Free Gospel Deliverance Temple, under the leadership of the late Apostle Ralph E. Green and Pastor Shirley M. Green. At the tender age of 9, Missy gave her life to Christ and immediately she was filled with the Holy Ghost and the language of the Rhema.

As she matured in Christ and the spirit of God began to pull on Missy and led her to the "Healing…. the Children' s Bread" under Ministers' Jonathan and LeCora Taylor , and "Victory Christian Church Int'l" under Pastor Dwayne Brewington in Gaithersburg, MD. She was taught how to mediate on the word of God, and understand the manifestation of healing power. In 2012, she successfully completed a 2 year discipleship course, which catapulted her into ministry. Many are called, but few are chosen (Matthew 22:14). "God's Chosen Child" was given a license to spread the Gospel as an Ordained Minister in 2013 by Pastor's Wayne & Michelle Green "Armor of Light Christian Worship Center."

The Lord allowed her visions to come to pass and a beautiful Children's Ministry was launched "Children of Destined Beginnings Learning Center" located in Clinton Maryland. Nicknamed, Destined Beginnings, this Christian-based educational center, is a home away from home for the children that attend. Missy welcomes and loves each child at her center; focusing on core biblical principles, based upon: "The Fruit of the Spirit" (Galatians 5:22-23).

God continued to pour into Minister Missy and after a series of life events, she stepped out on faith and established an Outreach Ministry, "Royalty." Royalty's mission stems from 1Peter 2:9 - A royal priesthood (Kings & Queens) speaking into the lives of a chosen generation: teaching the good news, comforting the broken-hearted and setting the captives free.

Committed to the call, this loving woman of God is an amazing wife, mother, grandmother, mentor, counselor, motivational speaker, evangelist, teacher and preacher; with an Apostolic call on her life. In light of all the recognition she has received, her primary purpose is to serve.

LATRICIA JACOBS

Made in the USA
Middletown, DE
02 July 2020

THE FIGHT OF MY LIFE

Do you ever wonder about God? Whether he exists? Does God love us? Does he hear our voice? Does he have great things in store for us? What is HIS plan for our lives? Who are we, that makes God want to use us to fulfill a purpose? What is that purpose? Do we have a say so? How much is required of us? Will we come out victorious?

Go with *Lady M* on her personal journey, as she takes you through testaments of her life. Sharing with her readers how she found the answers to these questions and more. In this inspiring story of faith, family, love, healing, and ministry, in-the-midst of abuse, loss, and challenges. A testament of overcoming and much more. Travel through each round with *Lady M*, as she presents her story in a way that will impact change, and encourage you to reflect on your own personal relationship with God. *The Fight of My Life* will show you just how real God is, and that no matter what battle you're fighting; God is with you and you too shall overcome.

The Fight of My Life will teach you to fight back even when life knocks you down, because with God you already have the victory.

9 780578 695280

COVERED
BRIDGES of
MADISON COUNTY
IOWA

A Guide

Andrew R. Howard